BLIND PUPPY FIVE DOLLARS

A Joyous Memoir of a
Rescued Golden Retriever

Loretta Scott Miller

© Copyright 2007 by Loretta Scott Miller
Photographs by Loretta Scott Miller

ISBN # 978-0-9788785-1-1

All rights reserved. No part of this book may be reproduced or transmitted in any form or by any means, electronic or mechanical, including photocopying, recording, or by an information storage and retrieval system, without permission in writing from the copyright owner.

This book was printed in the United States of America.

Shannon Road Press
Los Gatos, CA
www.shannonroadpress.com

ACKNOWLEDGEMENTS

IT IS CUSTOMARY to thank those people who have made a major contribution to the successful completion of a book, and this is as it should be. However, I would first like to thank some individuals whose contribution was to the full and joyous life of a rescued golden retriever.

Thank you to Northern California Golden Retriever Rescue (NGRR) volunteers Pam Lavin, Carol Frank, and Shirlee Thomas, in particular, and to all the other volunteers of this fine organization. Special thanks to Doctors Aurora Bibb and Joanne Williams and Veterinary Technician Kathryn Taylor – you were there when needed, from beginning to end.

I would also like to thank Jim Wheldon, neighbor and photographer, who shot the only known photograph of Cooper and *Baby* and let me use it for the Chapter Four heading. And finally, thanks to my husband, Todd, who not only put up with me while I was in the throes of writing this book, but made a major editorial contribution to same.

Thanks, Eddie.

February, 2007
Los Gatos, CA

AUTHOR'S NOTE

A word about the title and subtitle. ***Blind Puppy Five Dollars*** will be explained in the first chapter. I consider this book a *memoir* for reasons touched upon in the **Foreword**. I did not ask Todd to do a *read through* until I had finished the first draft, and being on a rather tight schedule, I had already done the cover art and had bookmarks made up.

Todd is an especially good editor and in most cases I agree with him 100%. In a case where I don't, I still consider what he has to say *very* carefully because, though hard to admit, he is nearly always right. He did not like my subtitle, A Memoir of a Rescued Golden Retriever. He felt I needed something that conveyed this was not a sad book, given the main title, and thought my subtitle was too passive. After disagreeing with him, I gave it a lot of thought. And took his advice.

FOREWORD

MEMOIR IS NOT a word usually associated with a dog. In this case, however, it is appropriate because the general rule rarely, if ever, applied to him. His name was Cooper, and though no smarter or more beautiful than the majority of golden retrievers, he was weird, odd, crazy, and extraordinarily goofy. He knew how to have a good time, and in doing so he made me laugh every day. Like a number of notables about whom glowing words are written he died too young, but he left a brilliant trail of unique and visually stunning memories which I have tried to capture in these pages.

Cooper came to us through the Northern California branch of Golden Retriever Rescue, one of hundreds of such non-profit organizations dedicated to saving a particular breed, or just plain mutts. I will not bore or depress you with statistics regarding the annual numbers of unwanted, displaced, and abused dogs. It's enough to say those numbers are much too large. The folks who work in these groups devote uncounted hours of effort and expertise for a single selfless motive — love. This book is dedicated to them in memory of Cooper, whose story reminds us why all that effort is worthwhile.

TABLE OF CONTENTS

ONE *Cooper and the Wall*   1

TWO *The Belling of Cooper*   15

THREE *The Ball*   25

FOUR *Baby*   33

FIVE *Cooper and the Boat*   39

SIX *Cooper as Watchdog*   51

SEVEN *The Hall*   59

EIGHT *Cooper Couch Potato*   65

NINE *Golden Naps*   75

TEN *The Arrival of Bigbear*   83

ELEVEN *On The Road*   99

EPILOGUE   113

ONE

Cooper and the Wall

THIS IS COOPER'S story, not mine. Still, a bit of background is necessary to set the stage.

I joined Northern California Golden Retriever Rescue (NGRR) in the fall of 1999 because of Boomer, our first golden, who died of old age that October. Boomer had been rescued by us, though not officially. We found him in the parking lot of the marina where we kept our boat; he was collarless, scruffy, and obviously abandoned. He was nearly starved and quite old. His face was white and he was deaf. I knew from looking at him he was a golden retriever, but that was all I knew about goldens then — what they looked like. When I called the local humane society to report a lost dog, they referred me to golden rescue and that's how I learned of their existence. We returned home to Los Gatos, in the south San Francisco Bay Area, often referred to as *Silicon Valley*, to have our newest family member checked out by our vet. He was underweight, but they said he would be fine.

Boom must have been twelve or thirteen when we found him, but he lived a very happy two plus years with us, and when he died I was devastated. To make it worse, I never even glimpsed a golden retriever after that. It was as though they had all vanished when I lost Boomer. I would have given anything just to say hello and scratch the ears of someone else's golden if I had met them walking in a nearby park or at the marina, but they were gone — all of them. In desperation I finally contacted NGRR and volunteered – to do transport at first – just so I could be around some goldens.

Anyone who has ever brought a puppy into their

home knows that a certain period of mutual adjustment is required. This is also the case when adopting an adult dog, especially one whose former life had a few bumps in it, as is common with rescue dogs. They all have a story. Some just a little sad, others you'd rather not think about at all.

Although Cooper was only one year old when we adopted him, he had already been *'thrown away'* twice. His first owners acquired him by means of a classified ad in the local newspaper – **Blind Puppy Five Dollars.** I later found out after taking him to the vet he was only blind in his left eye, from a birth defect. The ad was answered by a woman and her adult daughter, both of whom worked all day. And they lived in a condo. The Rescue volunteer who accepted Cooper into the system from these ladies suspected he was the product of a puppy mill – unscrupulous breeders who mass produce puppies for sale while keeping their breeding stock in appalling conditions (caged, dirty, neglected). Left to his own devices, and very little room, he naturally became way too much for these well-intentioned women to handle and was surrendered to NGRR at nine months old. Pam, the surrenders volunteer, told me when she visited for the first time Cooper (who's name at that time was *Stevie*, after Stevie Wonder) snuggled up with her on the couch. All he wanted was to get as close to her as he could, in her lap if possible.

Rescue found a seemingly perfect home for the pup — a nice family with three kids and a large fenced yard. After only three months, however, they too had given up and wanted to return Cooper (the name they gave him) to Golden Rescue. This is a stipulation in the contract signed by adopters; if they cannot keep the dog, for whatever reason, it must be returned to the Rescue organization for placement. No fobbing it off to Uncle Ned or cousin Sam or a nice neighbor. Rescue takes on the responsibility of finding a suitable home for each dog, even if it takes a few tries.

Once again, the problem was Cooper had been

left on his own. Both parents worked and the children were in school all day. Granted, he was in a large yard this time, but with no training or supervision he proceeded to chew his way through anything left within his reach. At this point, Carol, the placement volunteer, called me.

They knew my story, of course, and Carol was buoyantly enthusiastic on the phone.

"He's a year old and absolutely gorgeous! He just has this little vision problem."

"How bad a problem?" I asked, visualizing my golden bumping into furniture all over the house.

"Does he run into things or what?"

"Oh no, he just has trouble finding a ball if it goes into the ivy, stuff like that."

"You say this family has only had him three months? Why are they giving him back?"

There was a slight hesitation.

"He's destroying their back yard. They're gone all day and he's bored. He just needs some attention and training, which I know you can give him. You should take him to obedience school first thing. I really think you'll love this dog. He's perfect for you."

I was recently retired and could devote a lot of time to a problem pup, so after discussing it with my husband, Todd, who was dubious but agreed I should go see Cooper and take a few Polaroid shots of him, I set up a visit. On a Thursday afternoon in mid-June, the hottest day of that year at 103 degrees, I arrived at the family's tract home and was able to park in the shade. I had brought Bear, our border collie mix, with me to meet the youngster. She was a venerable lady of fifteen at the time, and though she had been the most athletic dog I had ever known in her prime, she moved a bit slowly by then and needed help getting into my station wagon. It was paramount that she and Cooper get along.

The mom of the family hadn't yet arrived home from work, so Carol and I and Bear waited on the front lawn under a large shade tree. When she arrived a few minutes later, we were all on the lawn introducing ourselves when the front door opened and the middle boy child, about eight or nine, emerged behind a — yes, *gorgeous* light gold retriever with the face of an angel — who was straining so hard on the leash the kid was nearly being pulled over on his face.

We were all invited in, thankfully, and I left Bear's leash on her, though she was perfectly behaved as always. She tried to remain a bit above it all, but this was hard to manage while a curious and devilish dog who'd been alone all day was trying to pounce on her leash. The older child, a girl of about thirteen, made Cooper perform the tricks she had taught him. He would sit perfectly. It was always his best behavior. On *stay* and *lie down* he was a little shaky. He had his own sleeping crate, where he spent the night, and the mother told me he went into it with no problem in the evenings.

"He'll do anything for a *jerky*," the daughter added, referring to a specific type of beef dog treat.

I took a few Polaroid shots and asked all the

pertinent questions, but it was just a matter of form. I was a goner when I first saw that beautiful face looking up at me on the front lawn in that peculiar way he had, because of the vision problem, of tilting his head and seeming to look over your right shoulder. I had to have him.

We were going to the boat that weekend, so I explained I couldn't pick him up until the following Monday, and in deference to Todd I told them I would give him one week's trial. This is generally not allowed by Golden Rescue, but since I was one of their volunteers and my husband hadn't seen him yet, Carol relented.

I was overjoyed until I got home and showed the pictures to Todd. After looking through them without speaking, he had one comment.

"That's not the dog you want."

Looking back, I must admit the Polaroids were not all that flattering; Cooper had that yearling quality, and with his big head and skinny legs looked more like a coyote than a golden retriever. We had both loved Boomer more than we had ever anticipated, and were caught in that grief-driven dilemma on getting another dog. We wanted a Boomer clone. When you're in that position, a mere picture – that doesn't even come close to resembling your former love – simply doesn't do it. It takes a face to face meeting to get you to realize that you'll never be able to replace what you have lost, even if you find a dog whose looks are close, because they all have unique personalities.

I had seen Cooper and fallen hard for him. Todd had only the pictures to go by, and they weren't really representative.

My marriage is one of the good ones. In more than twenty-five years I can count the number of serious arguments we've had on one hand and have fingers left over. But given the importance of this particular disagreement, we spent a somewhat chilly weekend on the boat. By Monday, however, I had obtained Todd's agreement, albeit reluctantly, to give Coop a week and see how it went.

When I arrived to pick him up Monday afternoon, I found him lying on the floor on his back, playing happily with the youngest boy. After loading his possessions in the back of the station wagon (the dismantled sleeping crate, some dry food, a couple of worn toys) I snapped the leash on Cooper and he jumped into the car readily enough, eager for a car ride. It didn't sink in until we were almost home and I stopped at a local pet shop to buy a choke chain. When I parked the car and looked in the rearview mirror I saw the saddest face I have ever seen. The expression in his eyes was clear . . . he had been thrown away *again*, by the three kids he loved. I wanted to cry I felt so sorry for him, but instead I assured him heartily that I would be right back (the sad face had changed to alarmed when I opened the car door and started to get out).

His sadness was replaced by intense curiosity

and great interest when we arrived at our house. He greeted Bear fondly and was introduced to Todd, who was charmingly reassuring as he always is with dogs. I let Cooper explore the entire house while still on his leash, then took it off. Carol had suggested I leave the leash attached to his collar for the first few days, but I really didn't see any reason to do that – then.

I had never been an advocate of the crate and Todd was firmly opposed to putting a dog in a *cage*, but because everything was new to Cooper and it was a safe place he was familiar with, we decided to put the crate in our bedroom, at least temporarily. Bear slept on our bed and I positioned Cooper's crate next to my side. It was a very tight fit. He slept in it all night the first night even though we left the door open (one of Todd's stipulations). Because our house is fairly small and the crate was huge, it lasted only a few days before being relegated to the back yard.

It had been many years since we'd had a puppy

and I hadn't given any real thought to puppy-proofing the house. After all, I was home all day, how much trouble could he get into with me there all the time? I was soon to find out.

Cooper at that age was a *power* chewer. If it had been football, he would have been an All American. He not only chewed on anything he could get in his mouth, he decimated it. What he couldn't swallow, he tossed in the air and caught, playing with the pieces of broken whatever. Stuffed dog toys were quickly shredded, de-stuffed, and the stuffing strewn around the room. To say he was *mouthy* is an understatement.

I got toys for him; sturdy, rubber, seemingly indestructible ones. He chewed them happily (well beyond their design limitations in most cases), but it didn't stop him from glomming onto anything else that was in his reach. Eyeglasses, Todd's cherished University of Oklahoma caps, one of my collectible Steiff teddy bears (he had one eye out but I got to it before he could de-stuff, and the eye popped right back in, thankfully). Pencils, Kleenex, underwear, you name it; if Cooper got hold of it, the item rarely escaped termination. It took about six months to train him to recognize what was acceptable chewing material and what was not. But it was in his first week with us, his trial period, that he achieved his magnum opus.

After his crate was removed to the back yard, Cooper usually spent the night on the carpet next to my side of the bed. He generally slept on his stomach with his head wedged between the bed frame and night stand, an often used position we would later term "docking," like a boat being nosed into a slip.

In that first week, he also spent a good deal of time on the other side of the night stand, with his head facing the wall under the air conditioning unit (an old one built into the wall that had come with the house). I thought little about this until I noticed he was *licking* the wall. By the time I checked it out, he had licked/chewed a hole, about three inches in diameter, in the drywall under the air conditioner. I was horrified. Not at the damage to the wall, but at the prospect of Todd finding it while Cooper was still on probation.

The damage to the wall was hard to see unless you were looking for it; it was only about six inches above the baseboard and mostly hidden by the air conditioning unit. But, inevitably, Todd discovered it. To say he was angry is not really adequate. He fumed, and rightfully so, over a dog that would *"chew a g—d----hole in the wall,"* but in the end he grudgingly repaired it. And Cooper, while not exactly forgiven for some time, was allowed to stay. It is Todd, after all, who has always said we can never foster a homeless dog because if it stays with us for more than a day, it's ours; he could never give it up.

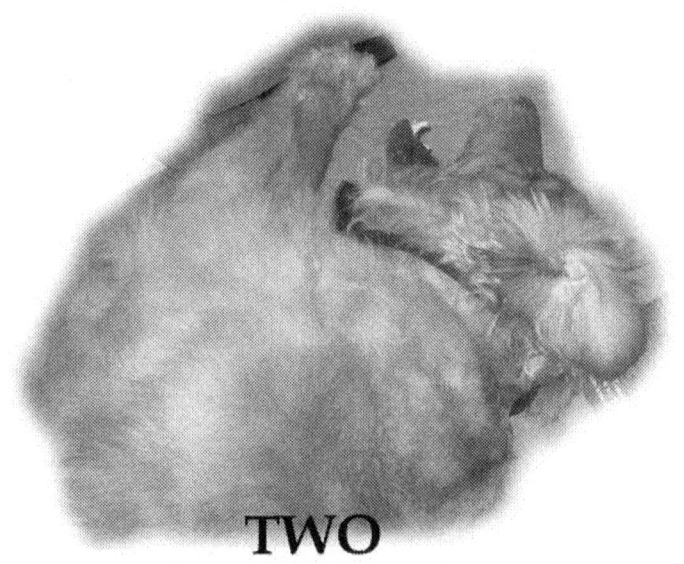

TWO

The Belling of Cooper

IT WAS OBVIOUS when we adopted him that Cooper could benefit from some basic obedience training. He had mastered the *sit* command the little girl taught him, but beyond that he was pretty much a wild goose. Besides which, I had promised Carol at NGRR that I would get him enrolled; sooner rather than later.

I found a beginners class through our vet and signed up for a six week course. Without going into agonizing detail I will just say it was only marginally successful. We weren't expelled, but when we emerged, the *sit* command was still the only behavior I could trust Coop to perform perfectly on a continuing basis. The real value I got from this exercise was learning what his *issues* were. Mainly, he was terrified of other dogs, especially when they barked, and very shy with strange people as well. At that juncture, a barking dog caused him so much alarm he would back up, slip his collar, and take off. Fortunately, the training ground was enclosed, but it was apparent I wouldn't be able to take him out on a leash without some failsafe solution.

He was also a consummate *puller* on the leash (when he wasn't scared) to the point he would choke himself and start hacking and coughing when wearing a choke chain. At about seventy-five pounds, he also had the strength to literally pull me off my feet (and I am not small). On one occasion, while on an extender leash, he spied a squirrel and took off in hot pursuit. Like an idiot, I did not release the leash, and when he hit the end of it, he kept going and I ended up flat on my face on the grass with a minor whiplash that gave me a sore neck for several days.

At our first lesson the dog trainer suggested I get a prong collar for him. These things look like something from a medieval torture chamber, but they are actually much more humane than the choke collar. They consist of a series of blunt-ended prongs joined by a loose chain and when the dog pulls, they contract enough to pinch his neck (which, I discovered on doing a little research, is what a mother dog does to correct her pups). It stops the pulling altogether, and they can't slip out of it and run loose, as Cooper was wont to do. A word of warning, however. Even with this type collar, a dog of Cooper's size and temperament, if running at full tilt, *can* pull you off your feet if you're not ready for it.

A Joyous Memoir of a Rescued Golden Retriever

We live just across the street from a nice local park which is a block wide and two blocks long, and has a playground, picnic tables, tennis courts, and at the far end a fully enclosed Little League baseball field. Just next to the park is a grammar school which, at that time had a large grass field and three softball diamonds as well. There is a winding asphalt pathway through the park and lots of grass and trees, with wooded areas along both sides. Dog heaven.

Although he was very spooky at first, I determined to take Cooper (with his escape-proof collar) to the park every morning. I walked him through and turned him loose inside the fenced baseball field where he could run and play. Cooper was very athletic and he enjoyed this freedom to run immensely. We went around 7:00 am when there was very little action in the park (and before the park rangers were on duty — leash laws, you know).

One morning we met two gentlemen with small dogs at the park entrance. John (with Abigail, a Scottie) and Greg (with Angel, a West Highland terrier). Both of these dogs were about Cooper's age – going on two – and being small, weren't threatening to him. We began arriving at the same time each morning to let all three dogs run in the ball field. Abigail liked to run a bit, but tended to be *above it all* most of the time when it came to playing. Angel was another story. She was young, feisty, and very fast. Cooper loved to chase her around the field and she was more than a match for him, zigzagging and cutting back to escape him, until they were both panting with exhaustion. They loved it. With practice, Cooper became very quick at the turns and zigzags, and we referred to Angel as his PT (physical trainer).

One of Cooper's oddities, which surfaced in this daily routine in the park, was his *circles*. He ran circles when he was happy, playful, or bored. Always in a clockwise direction, he usually started in a tight spiral, then let it take him wherever it would, expanding from the same midpoint, or whirling in the grass at random, like a spinning top. He would do this until he wore out, and then collapse on the ground, panting and grinning.

Gene, a friend of John and Greg's, joined us most mornings with his Abby, a tiny poodle mix. As word got around the neighborhood, other dogs and their owners began appearing until we had what we referred to as *the play group*. We had diverse breeds; from German shepherds to fox terriers; labs, poodles (toy to standard), a young border collie and even a pair of whippets. A core of around five or six regulars were there on a daily basis, and when the weekends came we often moved to the much larger grass field in the school yard to accommodate more than a dozen dogs and owners.

All, or nearly all, of the dogs were well behaved and sociable, and suddenly Cooper was the life of the party, forgetting his former shyness. He loved to chase the other dogs — he couldn't chase balls or Frisbees because of his vision handicap — and in his innocence he even chased the young whippets. Though he stood no chance against them, he was very fast and would have caught several of his other friends except that, in mid-chase, he would inevitably stop, turn 360 degrees, then start off again. It took me a long time to realize why he was doing that. The dogs were much smarter than I was, and had figured out that if they ran to his left (his blind side) he would lose them in his field of vision. He had to make his circle to find them again, then off he'd go, but they had gained a head start.

In the smaller group during the week, his playmates sometimes didn't feel like running, or they were engaged in other, more dog-like pursuits such as ball or Frisbee. If a few light nips at their heels didn't get any results, Coop returned to his first love; his solitary circles. It was wise to keep your eye on him because he was lost in the glory of it all. He cavorted like a whirling dervish, mindless of where he was, confident there was limitless space to do his thing. This was not always the case.

He had taken me down twice, while I was talking with one of the other owners and not paying attention to where he was. If you follow football, you will recognize the term *clip*. It is an illegal block in the back of the knees, and if you don't know it's coming, you're on the grass like a stone. If Cooper, seventy-five plus pounds of energetic motion, happened to hit the back of your knees while you weren't looking . . . well, he should definitely have received a fifteen yard penalty.

Everyone in the group knew Cooper, and knew his penchant for circular motion, but we had all become friends and had lively conversations on diverse topics while the dogs played. It was easy to become engrossed. The only safe place to stand and chitchat was against the cyclone fence so Coop couldn't get behind you. Nevertheless, people would gather in the middle of the field to talk and it was inevitable that tragedy, in the form of a great golden ball of fur, would strike.

I had been lucky; only my dignity was bruised when Cooper took me down. Some others in the group were a bit older or more fragile. In a matter of a few weeks, he took down two of our regulars. Everyone in the group loved Cooper, and his victims were more than gracious, but it was apparent to me something had to be done before there was a serious injury.

I decided an early warning device was called for, so I visited a locally owned pet shop. They carry all manner of unique items not found in larger, chain pet stores, and I found just the item I was looking for:

a miniature Swiss cowbell. It was brass, with a decorative leather strap that could be slipped on

Cooper's collar. It made a sweet, melodious sound that evoked mountains, meadows and streams; but most important, it was LOUD.

While some of the group continued to converse heedless of my unguided missile, I was always alert for the sound of Cooper's bell, and could shout warnings in time. From that time on there were no more *takedowns* in the play group.

Three
The Ball

FOR HIS FIRST couple of years with us Cooper and stuffed dog toys equaled imminent disaster. He loved them, but he just couldn't help himself when it came to finding out what was inside. He had, inherently, a very soft mouth; that is, he would take food from your hand with just the whisper of his whiskers and muzzle touching your fingers. No grabbing; no teeth. But the soft, fuzzy toys were irresistible to him. We learned this quickly and I solved the problem by getting him only hard, sturdy dog toys. One was a wooden dumbbell, the purpose of which was as an aid in training retrievers to retrieve, or so I gathered. To Cooper it was a chew toy. He would hold it between his front paws and gnaw on the squared-off ends. They eventually became rounded and he suffered no ill effects from ingesting the bits of wood he got off of it. He was apparently part termite.

Other items in his arsenal were tug toys; large, heavy rope with a tennis ball or some such thing attached. Coop loved *tug-of-war*, and he was so strong it was no small task for a woman to beat him at it. Dog trainers and behaviorists assert you should never let your dog win these wars in order to establish yourself as the *alpha leader*, but he was always so pleased and proud when he did win, prancing around with the rope in his mouth, trying to entice me into another game, that I gave in probably half the time just to watch his reaction.

In Cooper's second year with us, at the encouragement of my friend Pam at NGRR, I signed up to take him to the *Rescue Parade*. This is an annual event sponsored by NGRR in which rescued goldens and their owners participate in a parade during the lunch break of a dog show held at our local fairgrounds. It was scheduled on the Saturday of a weekend we were going to spend on our boat with good friends Emmett and Barbara, who also had a boat berthed at our marina which was about an hour's drive from home. The male contingent was uninterested in spending time at a dog show and arriving at the marina in the middle of the afternoon, but Barbara was enthusiastic about accompanying me and Cooper, so we arranged to meet the men at the boats after the dog show. I was relieved to have a helper going with me because although Cooper was by this time much more sanguine in the company of strange dogs, he'd never been to anything quite like this (nor had I, for that matter) and I wasn't too sure how he would react. Besides,

Barbara had a video camera and could record the whole experience for posterity.

We had to park in a large lot across a very busy street from the fairgrounds. There was a traffic light to cross to the entrance and by the time we reached it Cooper was pulling hard, even with his prong collar on. He was literally dancing with excitement. As we approached the building where the show was being held, he became a bit more apprehensive. There were scores of golden retrievers on the grounds, a much bigger crowd of people and dogs than he had ever seen. Barbara had been shooting video since before we left home, and I was beginning to understand how the rich and famous feel about the *paparazzi*. We found the check-in window for the rescue parade entrants and stood in line behind five or six other goldens and their owners. Coop behaved and did his *sit* well enough, but I could tell he was very nervous.

At the window we received a numbered armband for me to wear in the parade along with a *Welcome* bag containing a program (listing the name and story of each dog participating), small doggy items like wrapped treats, bandannas, etc., and — most important — *The Ball.* It was a large, multi-colored, stuffed soccer ball, and it seemed to have a mind of its own. It kept trying to escape from the paper welcome bag, which I was making every effort to keep away from Cooper until we got back to the car. Fortunately, Barbara was there to hold bag, purses, and camera during the actual parade.

There were probably twenty dogs for the parade, which consisted of standing quietly while you were introduced and the dog's story read over a microphone by the master of ceremonies, then walking around the show ring in front of a rather large audience. Cooper did quite well considering his nervousness; his only hitch was spying Barbara in the crowd (she had found a front row seat and was taping furiously) and starting off to greet this friendly face among all the strangers. It made a nice shot on the video tape.

When we got back to the car, Cooper insisted on having *the ball.* He knew it was his, and although I was a little concerned whether it would survive the hour's drive to the boat without being de-stuffed, I gave it to him.

"Just watch him, will you?" I said to Barbara. "If he starts to pull it apart, take it away from him."

But he didn't. He spent the whole trip holding it in his mouth or between his paws on the back seat, and when we arrived carried it proudly down the dock and onto the boat.

The Ball became Cooper's favorite; he carried it everywhere and not once did he try to pull it apart. Seams would split occasionally from normal playing use, but when they did I would sew them back up with yarn.

One of my fondest memories of Cooper is of him bringing me The Ball to play after dinner. It was a ritual we performed nearly every day. My part was to say "You bring me that ball!" and he would prance toward me carrying it, front legs arcing and high-stepping. I pretended to grab his front feet, one at a time, while he tucked them under to escape me and inevitably he would let the ball go to play-bite my hand allowing me to grab it and throw it across the room. He'd bound after it and the whole routine would begin again.

His love of the Ball spilled over to other stuffed toys, and after its arrival his de-stuffing days were over. He would carry them, sleep with or on them, but never again did he try to dismantle his soft toys.

A Joyous Memoir of a Rescued Golden Retriever

FOUR
Baby

THE STORY OF Baby is not a long one, but it deserves a chapter of its own because of its importance to Cooper. As I mentioned earlier, the park across the street had, in addition to tennis courts and a Little League field, a nicely designed, toddler-friendly playground. It was well frequented and as a result early mornings would often find a diverse collection of *kiddy* paraphernalia that had been forgotten by the little ones or their harried mothers the day before. Shoes, jackets, toys, drinking cups, blankets, you name it. Most of these items were either picked up later by their owners, or, more likely, trashed by the park maintenance crew on their daily rounds. There is a single lane parking lot at our end of the park which often filled up early, causing later visitors to park at the curb of the street.

On a morning some time after the advent of The Ball, when Cooper had decided he could play with his stuffed toys without dismantling them, he stopped at the curb after we crossed our street and picked something up in his mouth. It was the leopard *Beany Baby*, somewhat worn but in good shape, apparently dropped by a mom while loading her child into the car seat the previous day. Cooper wanted to carry it, but I took it away and stuck it in my pocket for safekeeping while we finished our walk and play group activities. Several times during play time he came over to sniff my pocket, making sure his treasure was still there.

True to his retriever heritage, Coop was in the habit of carrying something home with him each day when we left the park. The trash cans at the tennis courts always yielded up empty plastic bottles or tennis ball cans, which were his favorites. After bringing the bottles home, he liked to hold them in his paws on the lawn and chew the tops off (I was careful to see he didn't swallow them, and was mostly successful). This particular morning, as we stood at the ball field gate getting his leash hooked up, I asked, "Are you ready for the baby?"

He stood on his hind legs, dancing, until I'd extracted *Baby* from my pocket, then grabbed it from my hand and started straining for home. Nothing distracted him; he was on a mission. If people stopped to pet him he would allow it, but *Baby* remained firmly in his jaws. When we got home he dropped the Beany Baby on the step in front of the door. His mission was accomplished.

This became a ritual. I would carry *Baby*, always in my left pocket, to the park every morning. When it was time to go home, Cooper danced on hind legs until he had it in his mouth, then started off. The people we met in the park were charmed by this, although Cooper was oblivious to all the attention. They often asked me how I had trained him to do that. I sometimes tried to explain he had taught himself this little trick, but mostly I settled for saying, "It's just his thing."

The leopard was not so much a toy to Cooper as it was a cause. He rarely played with it in the house, so I kept it with the leash and bell to be ready for our walks each morning rather than in his toy box. Though he usually dropped it at the door on our return, once in a while he would take it inside himself and leave it on the floor somewhere. On one of these occasions, Todd picked it up and put it in the toy box. The next morning, *Baby* was no where to be found (it never occurred to me to look in the toy box; it didn't belong there). Panic ensued. I found a small bear to use as a substitute for several days, but it wasn't the same.

The leopard Beany had been out of production for some years I discovered, so I went on *eBay* to find another one. I did find one and won the auction, but while it was still in transit I uncovered the original in Cooper's toy box. The new one, complete with ear tag, is still untouched, but I rested easier knowing that I had backup if anything ever happened to *Baby*.

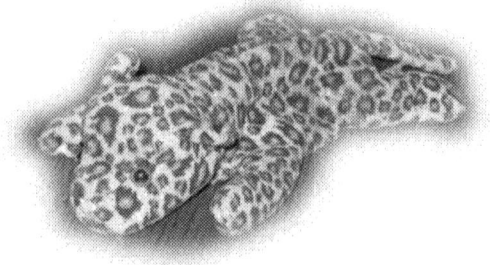

A Joyous Memoir of a Rescued Golden Retriever

FIVE
Cooper and the Boat

COOPER LOVED THE boat. He was a natural as a boat dog from the beginning. The boat was a thirty-eight foot offshore trawler, a life long dream of Todd's that we managed to acquire while we were still young enough to enjoy it for a dozen years. Since he was an inveterate snoop, the boat offered a treasure trove of nooks and crannies for Cooper to explore. He enjoyed going in, on, under, or around everything within his reach, and as strong and athletic as he was, that included most places on the trawler. Up the dock steps and onto the boat, into the main cabin, down two steps to the aft berth, up two steps onto the aft deck, up the ladder (with a little help) to the fly bridge. The only things that stopped him were the three steep steps down into the forward cabin.

With his one sightless eye, he lost depth perception; jumping down any distance always caused him a problem. I stored extra groceries in the forward cabin when we were aboard, including his treats and food, and when I went down there to get something for him, he would lie on the main cabin deck with his front legs dangling over the steps in anticipation. It was as far as he ever ventured in that direction on his own.

The trawler's deck was at least Cooper-wide all the way around. If he felt the need for exercise while onboard it was his habit to run, skidding around the corners, the entire circumference of the deck. He'd adapted his circle-running to include the boat. When we were inside the cabin, we could hear his toenails clattering on the fiberglass deck and see him streak by the open doors.

The boat was berthed on "P" Dock at the Pittsburg, CA, Marina, which sits at the convergent mouths of the Sacramento and San Joaquin rivers. These two rivers are the largest in California and have created a delta region consisting of over 1,000 miles of navigable waterways. This area, known as the San Joaquin-Sacramento River Delta, is located approximately fifty miles northeast of San Francisco Bay, and with its myriad rivers, sloughs, and canals is a boater's paradise.

There are twenty-four slips on P Dock, and we had many friends there, some of whom also had dogs. Blanche, a black lab, was a special friend of Cooper's.

Impromptu gatherings occurred frequently, but there were also more organized social events. An annual dock party was held in the summer, and occasional cruises with several boats to various destinations in the Delta or the Bay took place most any time of year. On one of the latter, in hot summer weather a few years ago, several P Dock denizens cruised to the *Willow Berm Marina* on the Mokulumne River for a Bar-B-Q and overnighter. Blanche and her owners, Dean and Julie, were among the group.

The marina is nicely appointed, with grassy areas, picnic tables with Bar-B-Q pits, and a rock-lined cove protected from the swift current of the main river. It was ungodly hot as is often the case in the Delta, well over 100 degrees.

When Dean said he was going to let Blanche go swimming, I decided to see if Cooper would like to join her. He'd never been in the water during our stewardship, but being so athletic I rather thought he would enjoy it. Especially if Blanche went first. We made our way down the rocky incline of the levee to the cove and Dean threw a stick into the water. Off Blanche went after it. Cooper was a bit more circumspect, but soon he was out there swimming with her. I had no doubt he would be a good swimmer, but because of his vision problem, I kept the twenty foot extendable lead attached to his collar in case he lost sight of where we were and the avenue of exit when he was ready to get out.

He had a ball. When they finally emerged we were all treated to an enthusiastic dog-shake shower, which, given the temperature, was not unwelcome. Back at the grassy picnic area, Cooper did several wet-dog circles, then crashed on the cool grass, a very tired and happy retriever. His next swimming adventure, however, was not nearly that much fun.

For those of you who may not be familiar with boats and marinas, the boat docks are constructed like the backbone of a fish. The *spine* is the main dock, and the *ribs* are the fingers which delineate each berth. P Dock was built of concrete; the main dock was about seven feet wide, and the fingers around three and a half feet. Depending on the size of a boat, this left from two to four feet of water exposed between the finger dock and the boat itself. If the boat is headed into the berth, which most of them are, more water is exposed at the main dock end because of the vee of the bow. This is all irrelevant under normal circumstances, but if you are blind in one eye, as Cooper was, your field of vision only catches one edge of the dock.

Once the dock gate was closed, other boat dogs would be allowed to run its length to get to their waterborne homes. Cooper stayed on his leash. More than once, in his excitement at being there, his left hind foot would have slipped off the blind side of the dock if I hadn't been watching carefully. If Blanche was on the dock, Cooper would start his circle running to entice her to play; this also spelled disaster in such close quarters.

Some of the boats had a gate built into the stern so you boarded by stepping onto the swim platform (a shelf on the aft end about even with the finger dock) and going through the gate. Ours didn't have the gate. We had to board using dock steps, a sturdy wooden structure with three steps which brought you up even with the boat's deck. Cooper conquered these steps easily; up three, turn, jump onto the boat. Getting off, he was a bit more cautious, but still confident; jump from the boat to the top of the steps, then down three onto the dock. Still, I always kept his leash attached during this maneuver in case he slipped. We necessarily did this several times each day; to go for our walk, up to the parking area so he could relieve himself, up to the car to go into town for supplies, etc. He was very good at it.

  At night, when we went to bed, I often left the cabin door open because Coop liked to lie on the deck or walk around it until he settled in for the night. It was the equivalent of his yard at home. I was reading in bed one night when I was overcome by a feeling of unease. I hadn't heard anything to cause this, but I got up to see where Cooper was and bring him inside. He was nowhere on the boat. I called, thinking he might have got off onto the dock by himself. Nothing. Glancing over the side, I saw a golden head in the water, making the turn around the stern of the boat, paddling steadily. He'd gone overboard.

The water in the marina varied from about five feet to eight or nine feet deep, depending on the tide. P Dock had twenty-four slips, twelve on each side, and we were at the end away from the gate, facing a city park about forty yards away across the marina channel. It had a steep, rock-lined bank that stretched away into a levee which enclosed the marina. There was no where there to get out of the water.

I started running for the other side of the slip only to see that gold muzzle rounding the bow; Cooper was swimming circles around the boat trying to figure out how to get back onboard. I called him and he swam right to me so I could grab his collar. While he treaded water, I yelled for Todd, but he was fast asleep as was most everyone on the dock. It was late. Coop weighed about eighty pounds at that juncture; plus he was wet. I knew if I could get his front feet up on the dock, which was a couple of feet above the surface of the water, he would help pull himself up. I grabbed the loose skin of his neck and shoulders and heaved with all my strength. After a few tries, his feet hit the dock and he scrabbled with hind legs while I pulled on the skin over his butt. He grinned happily when he was safely on the dock and gave me the shake-shower as I sat there exhausted. This time it wasn't welcome. It was cold as hell.

After I'd toweled him off and we were back inside I tried to figure out how it had happened. I came up with the following scenario: being such an expert at getting on and off the boat, Cooper, perhaps a little bored, had decided to hop off onto the dock and do a little exploring. When he did it with me, I always pulled the boat over as close to the dock steps as possible, but on its own, the boat would have drifted back a bit, leaving a wider space between it and the steps. When Cooper made his jump, I imagined, his hind feet had barely missed getting to the dock step, and he'd slipped quietly into the water between boat and dock.

Except for his territorial or watchdog alarm barking, which will be recounted in a later chapter, Cooper rarely made a sound. He never whined, barked, or cried about anything he should have. He was stoic. So rather than barking or yelping to let me know he was in trouble, he just started swimming around the boat. If I hadn't gotten up to look for him, he would have continued this until he was exhausted and probably would have drowned. There was no way he could have known in what direction to swim to get to a place where he could climb out on his own. It made me shudder to think about it.

From that time on, barriers were set at the dock steps so he would not be able to try that little trick again if we weren't around to watch over him.

Cooper's Boat

A Joyous Memoir of a Rescued Golden Retriever

SIX
Cooper As Watchdog

ANYONE WHO KNOWS golden retrievers will tell you that, although they have countless sterling qualities, goldens make lousy watchdogs. This is true. Goldens love everyone. As the old story goes 'if a burglar enters your house at night, your golden will hold the flashlight for him.' Also true. Cooper, however, was an excellent watchdog. That was one of his oddities. Of course, it was not without its downside.

Our neighbors in the house behind us had two dogs, one of which was a fence charger. If he heard us in our back yard, he would hit the fence, growling and snarling and clawing at the wood. Bear, our old border collie, ignored him. She was above such brutish behavior. Cooper, on the other hand, the first time he was subjected to this unprovoked assault, hit that fence like a linebacker. He growled, snarled, and scratched back.

I should have stopped him right away, I suppose . . . . Instead, I let him go at it for a bit. He hadn't started it, after all, and the neighbor's dog had it coming, the way I saw it.

Although he never precipitated action in the fence wars, Cooper did indulge in a little baiting. I would see him on our redwood deck, which was close to the back fence, lying on his stomach with front feet hanging over the edge, willing Duke to approach and make the first move. Or sometimes, he would creep through the flower bed next to the fence, hoping some small noise or his scent would alert the warrior on the other side. If Cooper heard Duke sniffing around, he crouched, ready to spring into action after the first shot was fired. In his defense, our neighbor did call Duke off if he was in the yard, but often he wasn't. After that first time, we called Cooper off as well. The fence was starting to take a beating.

I suspect Coop's proclivity for being a watchdog stemmed from more than a single cause. His one blind eye meant he lacked depth perception, which, when considering a potential threat would tend to make him err on the side of safety. If he couldn't tell whether a dog or its owner was on the street or had actually crossed into his territory, better to bark first and ask questions later. And his territory was very dear to him.

Given his background before we adopted him, it is easy to understand that when he finally found what the rescue folks like to call *a forever home*, he would have strong protective instincts toward it. Although he remained rather shy when meeting people or dogs while out on his leash, at home Cooper was a tiger.

We have three yards: a back yard with a redwood deck; a side yard with a patio, a small lawn, umbrella table, a Bar-B-Q pit, and flower beds, including what Todd calls *The Bat Cave* (a row of privets lined with dense ivy with enough room between them and the fence for a small boy or a dog to hide and let their imaginations run wild); and the front yard facing the park. The back and side yards are fenced. The front is open, with a large lawn, partially enclosed by a white rail fence, opening onto the driveway which extends the full length of the lot.

Blind Puppy Five Dollars

Cooper loved all his yards and enjoyed spending time in them even if we were not out there with him. He especially liked being in front, watching all the action on the street and in the park. Unfortunately, as I mentioned, he couldn't tell when people went by whether they were in his yard or not; so he barked. A lot. It's a busy street.

I'd set up a tether for him while in front, so he could only go about half the length of the lawn or drive. When we were out with him at a small umbrella table we had set up out there, I let him off the tether. If he started for the street we could call him back, and he didn't get tangled when running his circles on the lawn or playing tag around the cars in the driveway. But he liked being out there on his own as well, lying in the sun on the porch, until some imagined interloper caught his eye.

    We tried everything to curb his barking, to no avail. I hated to restrict his front yard privileges, but after two or three admonishments, he would be summarily banished to the house, head bowed in shame but spirit unbroken. Naturally, he would be given another chance the next day. While anyone walking by evoked a barked warning, there was one tandem that never failed to send Cooper into an absolute frenzy. It was a man who rode a bicycle with his Labrador running along beside him. There is apparently something about another dog running by that triggers a synapse in the canine brain, causing the release of great gobs of adrenalin. I was always glad when this guy zipped along in front of our house that Cooper was restrained on his tether. But one morning he wasn't.

We were about to take our daily walk in the park and Coop was sitting patiently on the porch while I fiddled with trying to attach his leash, when bike-dog guy went by. Cooper, in full voice, was down the driveway, skidding around the oleander at the street end after them before I could take a breath. When my heart started beating again, I began to run, screaming his name, although I knew I could never catch him. Horrible visions of his inert body lying in the street after being hit by a car flashed across my mind. But before I reached the end of the drive, still screaming, here he came, back to his yard, giving me a look that said, *"What? What? Why are you yelling?"*

It's the same feeling you get when your children have done something rash which puts them in danger; you are so glad they're safe, you don't have the heart to tell them how bad they have been. You just hug them.

A Joyous Memoir of a Rescued Golden Retriever

SEVEN
The Hall

WE LIVE IN an old house built in the early 1950s. It's rather small and we have way too much stuff, especially books. For that reason the hall leading to the two bedrooms and bath, which is a 1950s standard forty inches wide, is lined on one side with shoulder-high, one foot deep bookcases. A football player couldn't walk through it without turning sideways. My husband, Todd, who has pretty broad shoulders, barely makes it through facing forward. It's a tight squeeze, but we are used to it.

No one would think of a hall as being much more than a means of getting from one room to another, but when there's a Cooper in the house, the mundane takes on a whole new aspect. For example, after he had mastered the concept of what was off limits for chewing pleasure, he concocted *the game*. This involved finding a no-no item, usually underwear, socks being a favorite, and taunting us by standing in the hall with said item dangling from his mouth. His object was to be chased, of course. Stern reproaches were useless; a physical response was required. I'm sure there are proven ways to train a dog not to exhibit this kind of behavior. I must admit, however, that he was so funny when he did it, I did not try very hard to break him. Cooper was a prancer, and if you didn't respond immediately to his challenge, he would start highstepping toward you to invite a reaction. Front legs alternately arcing high in a crossover motion, his head up, sock or panties dangling from his jaws. It was impossible not to laugh. So much for discipline.

We did manage to scold Cooper for his misdeeds most of the time, and being sensitive, his feelings were easily hurt. When this happened he would pout. And he was very good at it. At night Todd and I would lie in bed reading or watching television, and Cooper was always there; if not on the bed with us, asleep on the carpet. One evening, after being reprimanded for some minor infraction, I noticed he wasn't around. When I looked in the hall, there he was, pouting. Head and ears down, long-faced, he was leaning against the wall by the bedroom door, his hind legs spraddled, his body boneless in defeat. He had sentenced himself to solitary confinement. How could you not laugh?

Our hall, besides being narrow, was very dark at night. There was a light switch in the middle, but by the time you reached it, you had traversed half its distance in inky blackness. On one fateful night I had left Todd reading and Cooper asleep on the bed beside him to go to the kitchen for a snack. I became involved in something – I no longer remember what – and was gone for some time. When I returned with a sandwich, switching off lights behind me, I entered the blackness of the hall confidently when suddenly I stumbled over a mountain and fell flat on my face. Cooper had changed venue; he was napping in the hall, no doubt so he would be the first to know when I returned. Although I cracked my knee and elbow pretty good, I was more concerned with having fallen on my poor innocent dog, who had nowhere to go to escape in such a confined space. Fortunately, neither of us were injured in the crash. And Cooper did benefit from the mishap in the way of snack food which was no longer fit for human consumption after falling on the dog hair infested hall carpet.

A Joyous Memoir of a Rescued Golden Retriever

EIGHT

Cooper Couch Potato

WE HAVE TWO leather couches in the living room which are nearly twenty years old, but they have worn well and look much as they did when we bought them. Beyond good looks, they also have the added convenience of not attracting dog hair. Long, golden, dog hair. This was an advantage because Cooper, from the beginning, claimed the smaller one as his own. The one where Todd sits in the afternoons, and I sit early in the morning, drinking my coffee, while Todd reads the paper in bed. On those mornings, Cooper would climb up on the couch next to me to snuggle. He would sit, leaning into me and I would put an arm around him. As I mentioned in the first chapter, he did this with Pam, the surrenders coordinator for NGRR, when she visited his initial owners who were giving him up. So it wasn't exclusive to the leather couches. Cooper's couch coziness was extent any time I sat on something wide enough to accommodate him as well.

On his first visit to our vet, he immediately joined me on the long vinyl-covered benches they provide in the waiting room. To say he was close was an understatement – he was nearly in my lap. So I put my arm around him to comfort him; he was obviously nervous. Kathryn, the vet tech and long time friend to our dogs, nodded when I introduced Cooper and told her he was a rescue dog.

"It sure isn't hard to see who *he's* bonded with," she said.

This was true. And on scary occasions like visits to the vet it was more than just being close; he would frequently turn to look me in the eye, all seriousness, the question hanging in the air as if spoken aloud.

"Is everything going to be okay?"

He was very much like a small child when it came to needing reassurance. Sometimes, in the middle of the night, I would be awakened by a paw gently placed on my side of the bed, and I'd look to find large, entreating brown eyes staring at me in the moonlight coming through the bedroom window.

"Can I get in bed with you?"

I would throw back the covers and help him up beside me, where he happily stretched out on his side, his feet near the edge of the bed. I'd put my arm around him under the blanket, and we were *spoons,* safe and warm for the rest of the night.

Under more relaxed circumstances, Cooper exhibited a full repertoire of sleep techniques. He was a world class nap taker; he would sleep anywhere, at any time, and in some of the weirdest positions imaginable.

A few years ago I put together a small book I called **Golden Naps**, illustrating this point. It was never published because the focus was much too narrow, but it is worth noting some of his odder napping habits in this memoir.

Since this chapter deals with Cooper's love of couches, I'll just show a few couch potato positions here. In the next chapter, we'll deal with napping everywhere else.

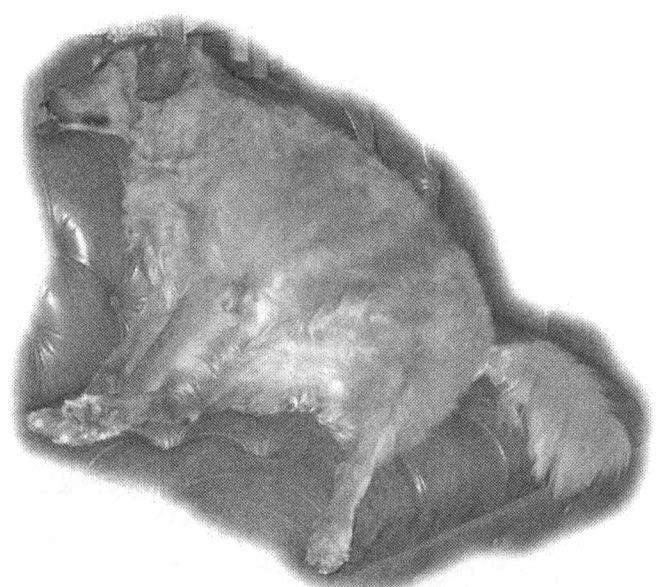

The Potty Sitting Nap

Cooper had the enviable ability, when relaxed, to appear boneless. He was also prone to spreading his hind legs wide while sitting, as if perched on a toilet seat. This prompted Todd to coin the term *potty sitting* to describe this phenomenon. Although he also potty sat while awake, the sleeping potty shows it to its full advantage.

Pillows of one sort or another were also an important item in Cooper's napping arsenal. In an adjunct to the Potty Sitting Nap, an alternate view shows the *Couch Back As Pillow*.

His stuffed toys (once he quit destroying them) also served him well as pillows.

Blind Puppy Five Dollars

True relaxation, in Cooper's sleep book, apparently required the ability to vary the position of his feet. This can be seen in the *Carousel Horse Nap*;

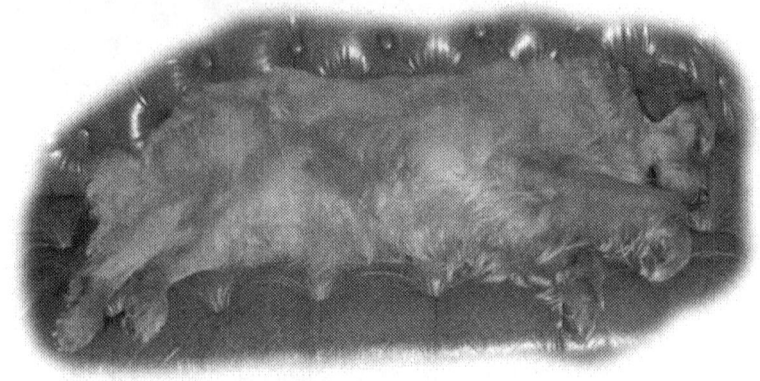

and also in the *Hang Dog Nap.*

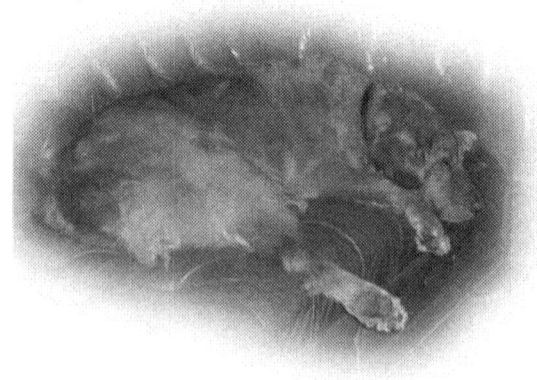

Cooper had many more couch potato naps, but it is fitting, I think, to close this chapter with the one that best illustrates his philosophy of life. As with everything else he did, Cooper pushed napping to the absolute edge, and got away with it.

A Joyous Memoir of a Rescued Golden Retriever

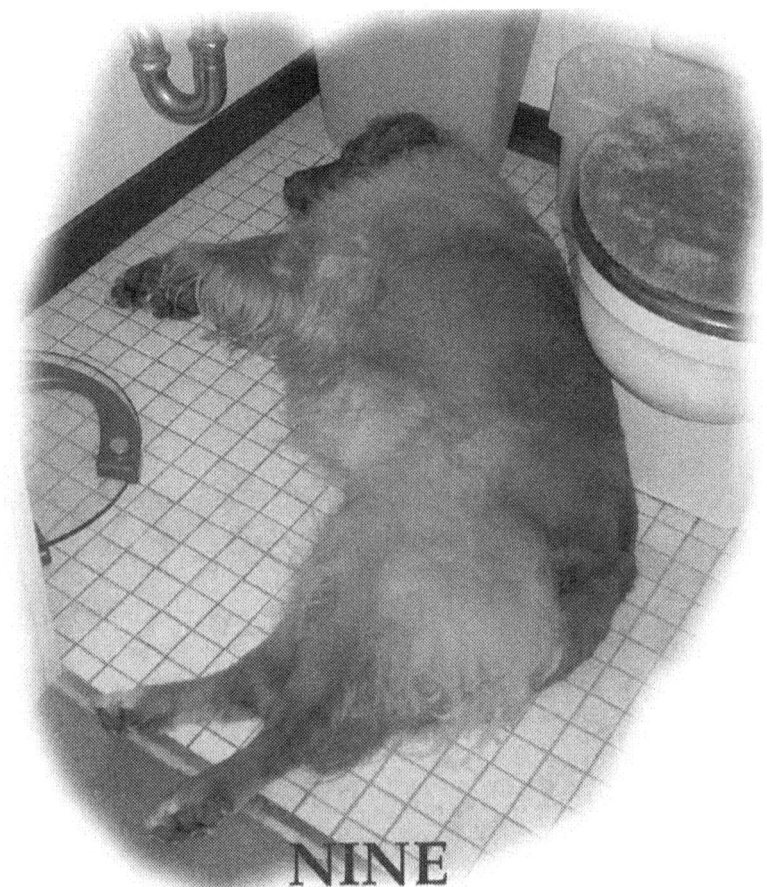

NINE
Golden Naps

WHEN IT CAME to napping, Cooper was never at a loss; he could sleep anywhere. And did. The nap zone shown here was our small half bath, and it became known as *Cooper's room*. It was one of his all time favorite places to sleep, I think because of the cool tile and also because of its isolation – no one could sneak up on him from behind. He spent a good part of every night in *his room*. It may sound strange, but lying in bed I could hear him when he settled down in there. It was a soft *thump-bump* sound as his weight eased onto the tile floor.

"Where's Cooper?" Todd would ask, as we read or watched television in our bedroom.

"He's in his room," I responded without having to get up and look.

Naturally, there were the more common locales for napping; in front of the fireplace, under an end table (again, to guard against the unseen approach of whatever might disturb his slumber), the middle of the kitchen floor when I was cooking, so as not to lose out on the possibility of dropped food. And outside, the wooden kitchen porch, asphalt driveway, and concrete patio apron afforded multiple areas for cat-napping while tethered and on watch. The lawn was also in his reach, but he seemed to prefer hard surfaces. He didn't do much sleeping on the grass. The dirt in the flower beds, however, was a different story.

As do many males of a number of species, he enjoyed getting dirty. One of his favorite pastimes was rolling in dirt, grass, leaves, and especially in anything that smelled really awful (fowl droppings in the grass at a large neighborhood park with a lake that was home to scores of ducks and geese springs immediately to mind). As a result, garden naps usually involved dirt of one kind or another.

The following illustrates what was known as *The Fern Face Nap*.

Also found under the loose category of *dirty, small space, yard naps* was the **Freshly Weeded Flowerbed Squeeze,** between a rose bush and a lime tree.

But Cooper's native ability to fit his large, golden retriever body into small spaces was never more apparent than on the boat.

He had his own life jacket which I put on him anytime we were underway. Going over the side into the river or the bay would have been traumatic, but he would have stayed afloat until we could circle back and pick him up. He loved to be out on deck when we took the boat out, smelling the breeze and letting it riffle his fur. He was not that fond of the life jacket; it was cumbersome and that's why I didn't make him wear it when we were docked. It didn't keep him from napping on the fly bridge, however, if he felt the call.

Of course where sufficient room existed, he took full advantage of it.

For example, on the bow.

Or the aft step.

But when space was limited, adjustments had to be made. Cooper had no problem with this. If he felt like sleeping, he dropped where he was. Which leads us to the all time number one *golden nap* in the category of ingenuity – and my personal favorite –

The Port Side Squeeze

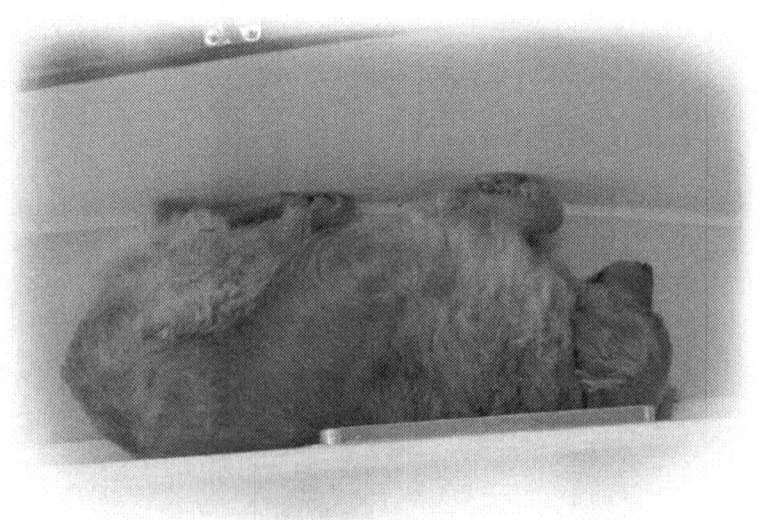

Blind Puppy Five Dollars

TEN

The Arrival of Bigbear

COOPER HAD BEEN with us for four years, most of which time he had also been the *only child*, when another golden retriever in need of rescuing came to my notice.

As a volunteer with NGRR, I received the weekly *Available Dogs* list so that I could match goldens up for adoption with families of potential adopters for whom I had done a home visit. On the adoption application, those looking for a rescued dog are asked to specify the age, sex, etc., of the golden they would prefer. As you might expect, most people are looking for a young, nearly perfect dog. Unfortunately, not many falling into that category come our way. So when I talk with potential adopters, I try to broaden their criteria, especially when it comes to age; from two years old or less to three or four, for example. I have been successful in placing a number of homeless goldens with loving new families and this is a very rewarding experience. The downside is having to review the *Availables* every week. Some of their stories make me want to cry, and the photos sent along with the emails, many taken in shelters where the dogs are currently being held, are enough to break your heart. I want to adopt them all.

      Senior dogs, seven or eight and older, are especially hard to place, as are the ones with medical problems. People often, I am ashamed to say as a member of the human race, surrender their aging pets because they simply do not want to put up with the care and expense required when their dog gets old. I have never been able to understand how anyone can give away a lifelong friend just to avoid the bother they have become. But it happens. More often than I care to think about. And NGRR accepts them all; no golden is ever refused, no matter what its problems may be. Medical needs are seen to, from required surgeries to hospice care, and the seniors are found homes or fosters, often from the ranks of our volunteers.

In the spring of 2004 I had been following the case of a golden from the Sacramento area who was being surrendered because he had been diagnosed with Addison's Disease and his owner refused to pay for the daily medication he required. Addison's, a condition also found in humans (John Kennedy had it), is a malfunction of the adrenal gland wherein the body's required amount of cortisone is not produced and must be furnished via daily pills, which are very expensive. This owner had acquired *Butch* (his name at the time) when he was a puppy, and had him for more than seven years.

I followed this dog's lack of progress for several weeks on the *Availables* list, and even tried to place him with one of my families with kids because he was said to be especially good with children. But they declined. I also talked with Shirlee, the Sacramento volunteer who was handling his surrender; she was getting more and more desperate to find him a home, and had paid for his medication herself since his owner would not.

"I've got to get him out of there," she told me on the phone, referring to his current owner's home. She would have taken him herself, but she already had four dogs and no more room.

"I'm going to bring him to the *Wag N' Walk* to see if we can at least get him a foster."

Shirlee was referring to an annual fund raising event sponsored by NGRR each spring. Held at a very large park in the East Bay, it's kind of like a county fair for golden retrievers and their owners. There's the walk itself, around a lake, a raffle for prizes, booths with golden-themed items of clothing, etc., for sale, and a planned program featuring rescued goldens and their adopters. Several available dogs are also on hand, so potential families can meet them in person.

It was at this juncture that I decided to share my concern about Butch with Todd. I explained that given his age and medical problems, it was highly unlikely that we would be able to find someone to adopt him.

"Well, what's going to happen to him?" he asked.

"I really don't know. They're taking him to this gathering in Pleasanton, but if no one decides to adopt him, I don't know what will happen to him."

If possible, Todd is even more soft-hearted about dogs in trouble than I am. He never wanted to hear any of the stories I read every week about abandoned and displaced goldens; it made him feel too bad. But I felt he needed to hear this one.

"You'd better go up there," he finally said, "and if nobody takes him, you bring him home."

And so, in late May, Cooper and I piled into my station wagon and headed North to the *Wag N' Walk*. It was a cold, gray, blustery day and I was not looking forward to the trip. Although Cooper had become a party hound in his own circle of dog and people friends, he was still not comfortable in large crowds of strangers (human and canine), especially if there was a lot of barking going on. I had never been to one of these events and wasn't sure how well attended they were until I got to the parking lot. There were literally hundreds of people, each with at least one, often two or three, golden retrievers; and they all seemed to be barking at the same time. Cooper was appalled.

Fortunately, he was wearing his escape-proof collar. He walked as close to me as he could possibly get as we skirted the perimeter of the active scene, avoiding as many of the barking dogs as possible. We finally settled at a picnic table at the far end of the grassy field where we could watch the action but not be in the midst of it. Cooper hopped onto the bench and leaned into me for a while, then moved up onto the table where he could look me straight in the eye.

I spotted the area where the available dogs were being held, not too far from where we sat. Wire mesh fences were being set up on the grass to enclose each golden, but give them room to walk around or lie down. The program to introduce these available dogs was progressing in the middle of the field, where each handler paraded her charge while the master of ceremonies told the audience about each dog over a microphone. I finally heard the name of the one I was looking for and saw Shirlee leading him around the ring. He was huge.

I don't recall his size being mentioned in the *up for adoption* listing, and the only picture available was just of his face. So it came as something of a shock. I later found out, in his first checkup with our vet, that he was a giant. Another glandular abnormality, it caused his bones to be elongated so that he was taller, longer, and narrower than an average golden.

He had a beautiful thick golden coat, but his tail had been shaved, so he was holding it down between his hind legs. Shirlee had told me she was taking him to be groomed the day before the event, and the only reason a groomer would shave a golden's tail is if it was so dirty and matted it was beyond combing out. I began to see why she was so eager to get him away from his current owner. I'm glad to report that when his tail finally grew out it was as magnificent as the rest of him.

When the formalities were over, the dogs were led to their respective stations to be on view, and Cooper and I went over to introduce ourselves to Shirlee and meet Butch. He was friendly enough, but it was obvious he was confused about what was happening to him. When the festivities were wearing down and no potential adopter had shown any interest in Butch, Shirlee helped me load him into the station wagon and we set off for home. I had agreed only to foster him at this point, but we both knew where that would lead.

Todd had about the same initial reaction to Butch's size as I had, but was immediately sympathetic to his plight. And within a matter of days, this funny, giant bear had become the love of his life. We have had several dogs and have loved them all, but there are those that get inside your heart in a particular way and you have no say about it. It was that way with me and Cooper. And for Todd, it was this giant homeless golden (he immediately renamed him *Bigbear*, both in recognition of his size and in tribute to our beloved border collie, Bear).

Bigbear was the antithesis of Cooper. Where Cooper was a bit shy, Bigbear was gregarious. Where Cooper was the strong, silent type, rarely making a sound except for his *watchdog* barking, Bigbear was a sparkling conversationalist. He had a vast vocabulary of whines, growls, squeaks, groans, and sighs, most of which had very specific meanings once you got to know him. But he rarely barked, unless barked at first. Then he was a lion. During his first experience of the *fence wars*, while Cooper attacked the fence in his usual manner, Bigbear let fly with the deepest, loudest, most ferocious sounding barks I had ever heard. They stunned the neighbor dog into silence.

And, of course, there was the comparative size; at one hundred twenty pounds, *"Bigbear makes Cooper look like a Chihuahua,"* in Todd's words. A slight exaggeration, but you get the point.

Despite their differences, Cooper and Bigbear got along quite well. Cooper's toy box was kept in the living room, and when Bigbear arrived with several very large stuffed toys, I set out another box for his. Naturally, Cooper went immediately for the new (different) toys in Bigbear's toy box, and vice versa. But there were no instances of possessiveness about their toys. The only disparity was if Bigbear wanted a toy Cooper had possession of, Coop would let him take it. He was very laid back. Not so Bigbear. What he had, he kept, but in a stubborn way, rather than an aggressive one.

  Cooper deferred to Bigbear in nearly all things, and Bigbear, being highly intelligent, accepted this deference as his due. Only when it came to food did Cooper stand his ground, but again, without any kind of aggressive behavior. Neither ever tried to take food from the other; it was only a question of who got his dinner bowl or treat first. Since I dispensed dinner bowls, I made sure Cooper got his first because he had seniority in the household. Bigbear waited politely, if not patiently, for the few seconds it took me to turn and give him his food at his feeding station.

Where treats were involved, both Todd and I handed them out, but Cooper managed to wedge himself into first place in most instances. The favorite treat of both dogs were dried chicken breast strips, which we called *chickies*. This was a magic word to them. The package of chickies was always kept in the same place – a cupboard on the left side above the kitchen sink. When the magic word was spoken, both dogs hurried to the kitchen, but Cooper always beat out Bigbear by putting both front paws on the counter. This was a long-standing trick of his, and the only time I allowed him to *counter surf.*

(As a side note, although Cooper was usually very good about not sneaking food from places he knew he shouldn't, on one occasion temptation got the better of him. I was unloading groceries and placing the full bags in the kitchen, making sure those containing tempting items – such as packages of meat – were on the counter out of reach. One bag I thought safe was left on the floor. It contained canned items and a loaf of

French bread sticking out the top. When I came in from the car with the last load, I found that the fresh bread had been delicately and precisely chewed off even with the top of its wrapper. The culprit was nowhere in sight.)

The chickie competition extended into our bedroom most evenings as well. It was our habit to have a late night snack while watching TV in bed, and when I went to the kitchen to prepare it, both bears followed closely (*bears* is a term Todd uses to describe the good guys of any species). Each of them got one treat in the kitchen, and I would take two more back with me so they could have a snack when we did. When I had food in hand and the kitchen light went out, Cooper would run ahead of me down the hall, and Bigbear was right behind me, stepping on my heels in his excitement. I would see Coop round the turn into the bedroom, tail flying high, and I knew when I got there I would be treated to the same scene that he enacted every night.

As I turned in the door, there was Cooper standing on his hind legs, front paws dangling, ears up at full alert, dancing slightly on his toes. He was making himself taller than Bigbear so he would get the coveted first chickie. He was my beautiful *dancing bear*. This sight never failed to make me laugh as I awarded him his prize.

In spite of his size, Bigbear was quite fragile. As a result of his gigantism, he was tall but narrow-hipped, and could easily be knocked down. He had very little muscle mass in his hindquarters, and his lower spine was fused so that it was difficult for him to get up once he was down. Most of his weight was in his chest, which was massive. In spite of his physical handicaps, Bigbear loved going to the park every day. I don't think he had been taken out for walks in his former life, and his excitement at the prospect was boundless.

With two large dogs to walk, I decided to get a double lead hookup, which allowed me to hook both of their collars to a single leash. Although outweighed by forty pounds, Cooper was strong and athletic enough to hold his own against Bigbear's frailty, so it worked out pretty well. When Bigbear started off in a particular direction, Cooper would go along truculently until he'd had enough of being pulled; then he would adopt his mulish look and set his feet. Bigbear was stopped, and Cooper led the way for a while.

The playgroup was another new experience for Bigbear, and while he enjoyed meeting new people, he stayed pretty close to me while Cooper was out turning circles or chasing the other dogs. A playful dog could knock him down very easily, and he knew his limitations. He was most in his element, however, at the playground. He loved small children and went out of his way to greet them, nuzzling their necks and making them giggle. Cooper allowed himself to be petted in these situations while he held *Baby* firmly in his mouth, but Bigbear encouraged and reveled in it.

For all their differences Cooper and Bigbear were friends, and once established, our two dog household moved along smoothly and without incident.

ELEVEN
On The Road

COOPER WAS VERY much at home in the car. He made himself comfortable and was the ideal passenger; no restless shifting about, no whines or barks. (In the chapter heading picture he was so comfortable he decided to stay in the car for a while after the rest of us got out – note the *potty sitting* posture.) In contrast to his territorial barking in the yard and occasionally on the boat, he never barked at anyone or anything while in the car. I could take him anywhere, and I did.

Our town of Los Gatos is a dog-friendly one and pets are welcomed by many of its merchants as long as they are on-leash and behave themselves. Some, like the local Ace Hardware Store, even set out bowls of water and have dog treats at the checkout counters. I always took Coop along when visiting Ace and for the most part he was a perfect gentleman. He was naturally curious and liked to sniff at all the strange objects on the lower shelves, but when we checked out, he sat perfectly and waited until he was asked if he wanted a cookie before standing up and putting his paws on the counter to receive it. The checkout clerks loved him and sometimes sneaked him a second helping.

He also enjoyed visiting the carwash with me. When we got out at the vacuum station, we walked outside the length of the building to the cash register in front, bypassing the gift shop. Cooper was well behaved, but the shop was cramped and full of breakable items just at tail-wagging height. In the small office in front, however, he was fine. There were a few chairs for waiting customers and a coffee bar, but nothing too delicate to be exposed to a golden retriever. Other customers sometimes brought their dogs as well, and on one occasion a women in front of us in line to pay had two medium-sized shepherds with her. As Cooper and I entered the office, she said "Please stay back; they're not friendly."

"Then why are they in here?" was my immediate response.

She didn't answer, but a seated customer smiled and nodded at me, in obvious agreement with my sentiment.

After paying, Cooper and I would go out to wait on the park benches provided in front. He'd climb onto the bench beside me and sit, watching the action. He got a lot of attention from other customers, especially small children with their mothers who asked to pet him.

Though a little reserved for a golden, he was definitely friendly and enjoyed being the main attraction.

When he couldn't go in with me, at grocery stores for example, he waited patiently in the car. I always left the windows down, and if it was very warm I didn't take him places where he would have to wait. But mostly he accompanied me, and while he was waiting, he usually liked to get into the driver's seat where he watched the passing scene out the windows. On returning to the car I often found people talking to him as they passed by. The grocery clerks who helped load my bags into the car especially liked Coop, who would hang over the back seat to smell the food items as they were placed in the back, panting and smiling.

On our local jaunts, Cooper always liked to ride in the passenger seat next to me while I drove. He would sit looking out the windshield, and if I reached over to pet him, he'd lean his head into my hand, pinning it to the seat back. He would hold that position until I finally had to pull my hand away to put it back on the steering wheel. It was the most loving of gestures; not meant to elicit more petting – that was impossible with my hand pinned – just enjoying the contact with me.

As a volunteer with NGRR I performed home visits to potential adopters in my area. This is mostly a happy task. The inspection of fencing and places in the home where a golden will spend his time is almost incidental to getting a good feeling about the people who are seeking to adopt one. I found taking Cooper along with me on these visits to be very revealing. It wasn't just to see how they reacted to Cooper, but how he reacted toward them. He was an excellent judge of character.

While most goldens are eager to meet and befriend everyone, this was not the case with Cooper. He was shy, as I've said, but usually took to most everyone eventually. There were a few times, however, when he absolutely refused to make up to some individual. When this happened, I watched that person very carefully. It never happened with anyone we saw on a regular basis. The one instance I remember most clearly was with a particular package delivery service driver. While Cooper would bark at anybody coming in our driveway, after I introduced them to him and told him they were all right, he would accept them, wagging his tail and acting friendly. But not with this guy.

I did my normal routine when this man tried to deliver a package, taking Cooper by the collar and telling him everything was okay, but instead of coming forward tentatively to greet him, he set his feet and kept growling low in this throat. The man actually reached out a hand and talked nicely to Cooper, but he was having none of it. I apologized and took the package, letting Coop stay where he was, but this happened one more time with the same driver. I sincerely doubt this poor man was a serial rapist or axe murderer, but for whatever reason he was on Cooper's list, and I decided I'd better take Coop's word for it.

So when it came to meeting potential adopters for our goldens, Cooper was my litmus test. He enjoyed these visits tremendously because he got to inspect new yards and houses, and most of the families were delighted with him. One man was kneeling down to scratch his ears when Coop turned and stuck his tail in the guy's face. When I explained that he was presenting his butt for a butt scratch, the man was a little startled, but complied. That family got their golden.

Another family was a bit on the reserved side. In the house, sitting on the couch talking with them, I kept Cooper off the couch where he was always used to sitting next to me because I sensed they would not like it. Although they were very nice people, Cooper must have sensed this reservation as well, because he was not his happy smiling self while we were there. He was very serious. These folks ended up buying a puppy so I was spared having to make a *yes or no* decision about them, but if I had been forced to choose, I think I would have gone with Cooper; I trusted his instincts.

For more than a decade Todd and I have made cross-country excursions to attend University of Oklahoma football games. OU is Todd's alma mater and we are both enthusiastic college football fans. We meet with old friends and it's a grand party for several days. In 1998 we drove back taking both Bear and Boomer in our station wagon. It was a memorable trip and both dogs enjoyed it immensely. In 2000 we flew back and Cooper, who had only been with us a few months, stayed in a kennel, but in 2002 we decided to make the drive again and take Cooper along.

When I was a child and traveled with my parents by car, we often took our dogs along. They were small terriers and I remember sneaking them into motel rooms under our coats because no one allowed dogs back then. Fortunately, there are now many motels and hotels that allow pets; sneaking a golden retriever into a room would be a challenge. The Residence Inn is one chain which allows pets, so we have stayed in their facility in Norman, OK (where OU is located) several years running. It is a large, comfortable place about two miles from the football stadium and has rooms equipped with full kitchens and living room and dining room space. The perfect party spot.

They offer two types of rooms; a studio design with bedroom, kitchen, dining and living areas in one large open space, and a double which is two stories. The doubles offer one bed and bath upstairs and another on the first floor along with kitchen, etc. On Cooper's first Oklahoma vacation we reserved a double because our dear friend Sheila, from New England, would be sharing accommodations with us.

There are ten buildings at the Residence Inn artfully scattered in a park-like setting of grass and trees. The double rooms are up a flight of outside stairs in each building, and Cooper found these to be great fun. He ran up and down these stairs, smiling, tail held high, looking back to see if someone would like to chase him. Except for the problems his impaired vision might have caused, Cooper would have been the perfect agility dog – the sport where dogs of all breeds run obstacle courses against the clock. He relished going up, around, over and under just about anything.

Though Sheila had no dogs of her own, she and Cooper became fast friends. I think one of the reasons she was a favorite of Coop's was that, being uninitiated in the art of living with a lively dog with a sense of humor, she tended to leave shoes and socks on the floor of her bedroom. Anything left on the floor was fair game in the sport of *catch me and take it away*. He would appear in the kitchen or living area with socks dangling from his jaws, dancing on both front feet, eager for the chase.

Sleeping arrangements presented another opportunity for Cooper to bedevil his new found friend. Todd and I had taken the upstairs bedroom, and although Cooper often slept on our king size bed with us at home, these beds were only queen size. There was room for the three of us, but it was a bit of a tight fit.

Never one to be uncomfortable if he didn't have to be, Cooper chose to look elsewhere after starting out upstairs with us. Sheila reported the next morning she was awakened in the middle of the night by her bed moving slightly, and when she opened her eyes found herself staring into a golden muzzle parked a few inches from her face on the other pillow. It was a bit of a shock, but she's a kindly soul, and allowed him to stay where he could stretch out in comfort.

Cooper's second visit to Oklahoma was in the company of his new housemate, Bigbear, in 2004. In the spring we had already decided we would get a new car before the trip and had pretty much settled on a Dodge or Chrysler minivan. With the arrival of Bigbear, the van became a necessity. We chose the Chrysler Town & Country, primarily because only Dodge and Chrysler offered in their '05 model middle seats that folded flat into the floor. This provided a large space which accommodated a huge rectangular dog bed where

Bigbear could ride stretched out his full length. That left the rearmost seat for Cooper, where he could sit like a passenger looking out the windows, or lie down for a nap. And the space behind the third seat had plenty of room for luggage. It is a wonderful van and I highly recommend it, especially for dog people.

Because of Bigbear's physical limitations of fused lower spine and weak hindquarters, he cannot climb stairs or jump up into a car. He can manage two or three steps if the risers aren't too high, but that's about it. The distance up into the new van was too much, so Todd built him a portable step (fully carpeted) which we took along with us.

At the Residence Inn we had to get a studio unit on the ground floor because Bigbear couldn't manage the stairs. Although Cooper knew which unit was ours, he often started up the outside steps on the building anyway – he had not forgotten his first visit and the fun he'd had.

Cooper was an *on the road* dog his whole life, enjoying new sights and sounds or relishing familiar haunts. He rode with his head up, taking it all in, never missing a thing. He knew how to have a good time and make every minute count.

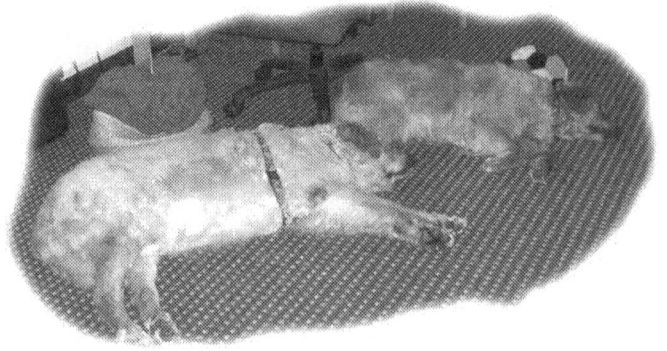

Cooper and Bigbear relaxing at the Residence Inn

A Joyous Memoir of a Rescued Golden Retriever

EPILOGUE

COOPER WAS DIAGNOSED with a brain tumor in mid-December, 2005, and he died on January 3rd. He was six years old.

I first noticed something was wrong in early December. Cooper just wasn't his normal, playful self, and sometimes he seemed to lose control of his right front paw; it would tuck under and he wouldn't or couldn't move it back. Then he would sleep for an hour or so and be all right when he woke. After a few days, I decided he was having some kind of non-violent seizure and took him to a local vet specialist. She examined him and immediately called the Neurology Department at UC Davis, the premiere veterinary school and teaching hospital on the West Coast, to schedule an exam and MRI.

We left the next morning in the dark to drive the one hundred odd miles to Davis, where the head of Neurology spent a couple of hours examining him. He was scheduled for the MRI that afternoon, and since it required a general anesthetic, they would keep him overnight.

The doctor called me late that afternoon to tell me he had a very large brain tumor which was virtually inoperable. They would keep him in Intensive Care that night and under observation the next day and if all went well we could then bring him home.

The vets gave us medication to control Cooper's seizures, but we were warned that they would get progressively worse as the tumor put more pressure on his brain. The pills did their job long enough for Coop to have a happy Christmas, even trying to play a bit with his new tug toys, but as the New Year approached, he began to go downhill. It was time to step up to the last, and most difficult, act of love.

Our long time vet came to our home to euthanize Cooper, and he died peacefully in my arms.

After more than a year, I am still not over losing him. I doubt I ever will be. But his life, though short and with a pretty rough start, was a celebration of pure joy. He never had a bad day, was always good-humored, and he could find the fun in just about anything. He had a solid gold life for a *'blind puppy'* thought to be worth only five dollars.

A Joyous Memoir of a Rescued Golden Retriever

www.ingramcontent.com/pod-product-compliance
Lightning Source LLC
Chambersburg PA
CBHW031254290426
44109CB00012B/580